Build your community for success

Contents

Introduction 3

How does one create a new community? 4

THE NEED FOR COMMUNITY 5

How do communities work? 6

Quran Julie Wang on How to Make
Workplaces Happier..7

What is a community online? 8

Create a Community Operations Department
within Your Team..9

Make a Space That Is Open for People to
Connect..9

THE ESSENCE OF RELEVANCE.......................10

Enhanced Customer Loyalty and Support....11

Why is it crucial to foster a sense of
community at work?......................................12

A learning community's advantages.............13

COMMUNITY ORGANISATIONS: HOW DO
YOU BRING ABOUT CHANGE?.......................14

Creating community as a businessperson ...15

Use memes, GIFs, emesis, and quotation
pictures. 16

Top tactics to increase community involvement 16

Benefits of a Community in B2B 17

How much time is needed for this? 18

If you're trying to make a difference in the world 19

It's simpler than you would imagine creating a strong brand community. 20

Be approachable and kind. 21

Online communities may significantly improve interpersonal relationships and customer experiences. 21

Provide a forum for users with various viewpoints...22

Best practices for building communities......23

Use effective community-building techniques 24

Are there any possible grants because I cannot afford this?.......................................24

Concentrating the mind 25

Plan your objectives....................................26

The needs of your users..............................27

Free Online Communities 28

Introducing audience to corporate culture..29

A community needs to change and improve.
....30

You want to produce content, not dialogue.
....30

For your online community, select a platform.
....31

Platform-related issues...................................32

Community Platforms You Own....................33

Engage your staff in fostering a sense of
community and culture...............................34

The next stage is to build a fundamental plan
....35

A brand community: what is it?...................35

Provide a Platform for Your Community......36

Conventions vary depending on the audience.
....37

Find a goal that all the members can agree
on. 38

A brand community exists to benefit its
members..39

Why Is Workplace Community Important? .40

Encourage Participation...............................41

Imagine a neighborhood as a tree 41

Do not forget that YouTube is a social networking platform. 42

Why virtual communities should be preferred to social networks 43

Just why Create a Brand Community? 44

Determine your objectives. 45

How can I advertise it?.................................46

Maintaining their participation is crucial after you have members in your online community 47

Make use of social media.............................48

Quality Should Precede Quantity.................48

Make use of brand ambassadors 49

Boost the lifetime value of each client 50

Consider the Correct Platforms 51

Execute every action in the step..................52

Companies that excel in community engagement 52

The next phase in an online community management plan is to keep growing your community 53

Speak Your Community's Language 54

For further control, use branded community platforms...55

Introduction

Rewards have the potential to be a potent tool for nurturing a community as it grows, but not all rewards are created equally for those fostering communities. You need to be aware of the two different forms of incentives. Intrinsic incentives come first. This technique validates your members' efforts without sending something tangible, as opposed to sending an actual product. This may be done via providing thank-you emails, VIP material access, public mentions, etc. Members are less likely to contribute just for the purpose of receiving rewards under this kind of reward structure. Extrinsic benefits are the second. In this scenario, you provide the members of your community tangible items like swag and other stuff.

A successful company is one that earns enough revenue to make a profit every year, to put it simply. However, building a supportive community around your brand, service, or company is a tactic that's frequently useful if business owners want to sustain that success over time. This encourages fan loyalty and enthusiasm by giving your consumers a space to communicate with you, your staff, and other customers.

But creating a supportive environment for your company takes effort and a well-thought-out strategy; it doesn't happen overnight. Ten members of the Young Entrepreneur Council offer their best advice on community development to assist.

How does one create a new community?

I recently offered six key lessons on this subject. But I am aware of your true desires: a simple procedure. How exactly does one create a community? How are you going to start it? What are the procedures?

I've chosen to offer my method for creating new communities from scratch because I receive this question a lot.

These steps have been used in every successful community I have started. I've discovered that, whether they were aware of it or not, the majority of the enormous groups you see today have also used these 10 stages to develop community.

THE NEED FOR COMMUNITY

In terms of us personally, our societal interests and general well-being are greatly influenced by our feeling of community. A group of people who share common interests may be quite strong. A common proverb reads, "It takes a village to raise a child." If the aforementioned "child" were a brand, hobby, or organization, it's worth would derive from the community it has cultivated around it as much as the product itself. Today, any product, passion, or business may benefit greatly from this community.

The community in a business setting may consist of customers, clients, and influencers. There is a lot of talk about "Influencer Marketing" right now.

How do communities work?

People get together in communities to exchange information, experiences, and stories with one another. They feel more connected to those who share their hobbies or passions as a result.

You could already be a part of a community, both online and off. But why is it so unique?

Involving your clients or other interested parties in the deeper meaning behind your brand is its primary benefit. By creating a setting where individuals may contribute their own thoughts, experiences, and knowledge, community aids in this. It also enables you to make your brand more than just a product or service, allowing your consumers to support the essence of your company.

Quran Julie Wang on How to Make Workplaces Happier

Quran Julie Wang, a civil rights attorney and New York Times best-selling book, discusses how she thinks workplaces might do a better job of fostering pleasure.

An organization's capacity to prosper and meet its goals can be significantly impacted by workplace culture. Additionally, many managers opt to go beyond enhancing workplace culture and instead foster a sense of community that encourages greater employee involvement. Reviewing methods for achieving this objective may be useful for you if you're a manager looking for ways to assist team members in developing more substantial relationships at work. This article explains how to foster a sense of community at work and why it's crucial to do so.

What is a community online?

Online communities are simply areas where people interact with one another. Online communities are frequently developed around shared values, beliefs, or objectives.

Your company objectives will determine the sort of community you create. For participants in a fitness programmed to share knowledge and transformation experiences, a community for a fitness instructor might resemble a personal Face book group. For a photographer, it may be a public area where thousands of people congregate, exchange resources, and comment on one other's pictures.

Online communities, regardless of the platform you use, are an effective approach to encourage deep connections among your followers since they provide your audience the chance to:

Create a Community Operations Department within Your Team

A community operations manager's duties include managing, tracking, and analyzing the information on your company's entire business effect. Community operations experts should continuously be searching for ways to enhance procedures, tech stacks, and platforms from the viewpoints of both community members and the community team. One may state that a community manager works on the community's front end, providing content, moderating discussions, etc. in marketing or development words. The community operations specialist is working behind the scenes to ensure data quality, integrity, consistency, metrics, tech stack, platforms, and that they all function together and independently.

Make a Space That Is Open for People to Connect

Although the word "community" is frequently used these days, one thing is certain: If you're not forging deep bonds among your followers, you don't have a community—you have an audience. It's critical to foster open communication among your members and to promote open discussion that doesn't necessarily centre on you or your company setting the agenda. Also keep in mind that a community is fundamentally a human desire since individuals naturally want to belong and feel like they belong. Remind your community on a regular basis how much they are cherished. Keep in mind that nothing can replace a face-to-face meeting. Online communities serve as fantastic places to exchange ideas and make new acquaintants.

THE ESSENCE OF RELEVANCE

Sharing a common interest is fundamental to what community is. In the end, the fascination transforms into the applicability to the unique circumstances of each person and the organizer. Relevance creates a connection and shared interest among the parties. It offers a focal point that speaks to a widespread, universal need or desire.

Individual enthusiasm is insufficient. Even if someone may be interested in a certain subject, if they are not enthusiastic about it, it may be difficult to maintain that interest over time. Does someone have the ability to make a substantial difference, even if they are enthusiastic about a particular interest? Expertise is not the same as interest.

Enhanced Customer Loyalty and Support

Over time, when your members engage with you, they will develop a stronger bond with your brand. Customers become more devoted to your company when they feel a feeling of belonging in communities. This is due to the fact that participants have an opportunity to participate and add their experiences, thoughts, and insights to the conversation.

Members will begin to feel like they have an ownership stake in the community and that it is their duty to make it successful when this occurs more frequently over time. This may result in more people promoting your good or service, which aids in getting the word out about what you do.

Why is it crucial to foster a sense of community at work?

In order for all internal stakeholders within an organizational structure to collaborate efficiently and feel confident in their respective responsibilities, it is crucial to foster community in the workplace. The trust, respect, empathy, and collaboration levels among employees are frequently greater in workplaces that successfully establish community. Following these fundamental tenets, the following are some particular advantages that may result from workplace community building:

Support systems: Workers who feel like they belong to a community may be more concerned with the success and well-being of their coworkers. Consequently, in such a setting, professionals could have access to a higher degree of support from one another, which might lower their stress levels and increase their productivity.

A learning community's advantages

Principal advantages of learning communities are:

Social learning: Students can learn in communities by assisting others and posing inquiries.

Faster responses: In communities, questions are addressed more quickly without waiting for an instructor response.

Ideas for creating courses: Our best course designers pay close attention to any queries or difficulties students may have. They make use of this data to generate new course materials or other offers by anticipating the demands of their students.

Cohort-based Learning: Cohort learning fosters the desired sense of community among students while also enhancing academic performance. Members gain from a strong network of allies and increased accountability.

COMMUNITY ORGANISATIONS: HOW DO YOU BRING ABOUT CHANGE?

Depending on where you work and your individual objectives, there are many different methods to organize your community. Each of the strategy-specific sections that come after this one include more thorough "how-to" instructions.

Nevertheless, regardless matter what your final objectives may be, some fundamentals remain essentially the same. Therefore, what follows is only a broad summary to encourage you to consider the essentials.

You must first and foremost include people in your community-building activities. This is where community organizing starts. You may accomplish this in a variety of ways, including through casual talks, door-to-door solicitation, and the use of more official recruiting techniques.

Creating community as a businessperson

Without outside assistance, busy businesspeople can entirely ignore their own requirements. Additionally, without connection to a fan base, a brand risks losing sight of its purpose.

For an entrepreneur, community may relate to two things:

a team of reliable peers, relatives, family, or other company owners who offer support, criticism, and suggestions to keep your operation running well.

a group of brand supporters and clients who are linked online by a common interest.

Community of both kinds is essential to an entrepreneur's success. Having a focus and an outside viewpoint might help the first group stay connected to the outside world. Your close friends and relatives may provide you with candid criticism without being engaged.

Use memes, GIFs, emesis, and quotation pictures.

Using GIFs, emoticons, quote pictures, and memes—all of which make up the vocabulary of the social media space—is a sometimes ignored technique to create a community. Your material becomes more interesting, relatable, and shareable when handled appropriately, and your brand gets more endearing. Last but not least, fans feel special when you provide them exclusive promotions. By rewarding them for their dedication and involvement, you are expressing your concern for this community. This is a fantastic example of how to reinforce behavior positively, and it nearly always results in improved brand affinity and continuing customer loyalty.

Top tactics to increase community involvement

Can you list any community involvement tactics that have been successful for you or some successes you've had while working at The Alliance? As I just said, content has always been and will continue to be a significant component of that engagement aspect. For some background, let's say that for around six months following the introduction of our initial community, Product Marketing Alliance, we didn't really provide any paid-for items. To ensure that when we did have those paid-for goods, people would have that confidence and respect for us, all we did was give blogs, reports, podcasts, whitepapers, and webinars for free.

Benefits of a Community in B2B Online communities make it easier for and promote interaction between your consumers and your business. Your business will gain from this in a variety of ways, including decreased support tickets, more customer retention, and the ability to generate new product ideas. Consider the B2B software supplier Info land as an example. By engaging their community, they were able to significantly enhance customer service and divert a staggering 40% of their support queries.

So, have you considered starting a community of your own? Here are our top ten suggestions for starting.

How much time is needed for this?

Everything is set up to accommodate your situation. We want your time in the community to be worthwhile in terms of the relationships you make, the lessons you gain, and the money your business will make as a consequence.

When you initially join, we advise blocking out a few hours each week to read through the information. You may do it on your own or through a live learning experience. After your first four weeks, you'll speak our language and be able to understand how to take advantage of the community and activities as they are happening.

In the long run, even during hectic periods, we advise taking part in our seasonal planning event four times year, visiting Office Hours once per month.

If you're trying to make a difference in the world, you know that it's a never-ending battle—one that may wear you out even when your job is rewarding and encouraging. You might need some time to take a step back, relax, and collect your breath in a space where you can spread out and look out to the distance.

We created the Windfall Resident Programmer in response to this. It has served as a haven of rejuvenation and retreat for those working for social change since 1989. Our main goal is to respect and support people who devote their time and effort to achieving a more equal society. If you've been working hard and need to take a step back to assess

It's simpler than you would imagine creating a strong brand community.

These fantastic brand communities all have the trait of being aware of the concerns of their target audiences. These 8 businesses have created a community centered on helping their consumers to live out those ideals through a comprehensive and fulfilling brand experience with this knowledge at the helm.

The biggest brand communities in the world give their members the resources to include other like-minded people in the brand's story, the inspiration to keep them engaged, and the power to spread the love as far as they can, whether it be through rewards, special events, user-generated content like newsletters or brand advocates.

There isn't much greater community than that!

Be approachable and kind.

Make yourself approachable, advises Heather Nix, director of marketing. Having direct connectivity to your community and consumers gives you an advantage over more established businesses while you're just getting started. Tell a relevant brand narrative and put your face in front of your company.

You could play a variety of responsibilities as a small company owner, such as providing customer service and providing social support. Keep in mind that your early brand supporters are crucial to the development of your community. Community manager Molly Milosevic advises businesses to take the time to get to know their social media fans and find out what else they might need from them in addition to their product.

Online communities may significantly improve interpersonal relationships and customer experiences. They primarily serve as a forum for knowledge exchange between people. Customers may have queries or issues that locals in the community can answer, thus this is especially helpful for companies that provide complicated goods and distinctive services.

Additionally, internet communities provide firms with useful input. Brand managers may gain valuable information about client preferences by routinely engaging with the community and asking for feedback in order to inform strategic choices that improve experiences.

A sense of belonging may also be found in online groups. Customers frequently feel more linked to the business and its ideals when they participate, which increases loyalty and happiness.

Provide a forum for users with various viewpoints.

If your company deals with a delicate or contentious subject, you should approach it in a calm manner by removing barriers of miscommunication and inspiring employees to be receptive to new ideas and opinions.

This is what daily's mission as a platform for the religious community is all about. Conflicting religious beliefs exist among people, even within the same religion, which can result in tense debates and deeper miscommunication. However, the website gives users the option to constructively share their religious convictions and views with one another so that everyone may have a better understanding of various religions.

Best practices for building communities

What would be your best piece of advice for those looking to form a community? Be tolerant. It won't take place immediately. It won't take place within a few months. It will take a while to complete. In the beginning, it may seem discouraging. It could seem like you're speaking into thin air when you're attempting to increase community involvement. The majority of individuals probably stops thinking about it at that point since they believe it to be a waste of time and will not benefit them. But if you don't stick with it through the first few months, you'll never build a self-sufficient society.

Use effective community-building techniques

Building a successful community strategy requires three key components: increasing traffic, promoting content production, and activating new users. Including links to your community on your website, in email newsletters, and on social media may increase traffic and encourage users to join. Download our free eBook on crucial community integrations for further advice on how to increase traffic to your community. Finally, improving the SEO of your community content will significantly increase the amount of organic consumer discovery.

Are there any possible grants because I cannot afford this?

Yes! We encourage you to submit an application for a scholarship if you are developing a community company but the full membership price is a barrier for whatever reason.

There are two varieties:

The other is intended to increase diversity in our cohort by encouraging people of color, those outside the binary gender spectrum, and others who are underrepresented in entrepreneurship to join us. The first scholarship is needs-based and is intended to assist anyone with financial need to attend, including those living in a region of the world with lower purchasing power.

Once you have been given permission to join BACB, you will be able to submit an application for a scholarship.

Concentrating the mind

Have you ever had problems concentrating your efforts on what is important?

The value that each and every member of your community receives from being a part of a vibrant network of people coming together to master something fascinating or important, together, can be generated by creating an online community. This value is magical, life-affirming, brand-affirming, and passion-affirming.

In a world filled with endless diversions where nobody has time to learn anything new, this focus is wonderful.

Plan your objectives.

You must first have a distinct understanding of your goals before you can develop a marketing plan. Building an online community is no different from this. Some people might assume that creating a community is really simple. Planning is essential, though, or you risk having a community that is disengaged and achieves no actual achievements.

Be as detailed as possible when setting your goals. This will assist you in understanding what you must accomplish as a business and the kind of material and activities you must produce for your members.

Among the objectives to take into account are developing sincere relationships, raising awareness, assisting users with the product, obtaining feedback, raising customer satisfaction ratings, raising sales, etc.

The needs of your users.

When creating an online community, make careful to take your users' requirements into account as well as the reasons your organization needs it.

What do individuals seek when they join a community? What are their prospects? Reaching out might be spurred on by a need for companionship, insider information, or solutions to a problem.

The secret to its success is building a community that belongs to your users, not to you. While you will benefit from this, in order for you to succeed, your users - and their requirements - must come first. You may, however, combine your organizational objectives with what your consumers will find useful.

Free Online Communities

There are "free" platforms like Face book and Twitter that provide aspects of a community, but using them has advantages and disadvantages.

Its availability to consumers at no cost and with an existing audience is a significant benefit. In other words, as long as you do the research to determine who on this platform you want to reach, you can set up an account, develop content, and distribute it to your followers for free.

The drawback, though, is that you don't actually "own" your community and are thus subject to the choices made by these businesses over how the platform distributes your material to others. The content algorithm changes just when you've mastered the platform your community relies on.

Introducing audience to corporate culture

To extend your values and culture to the people who are supposed to benefit from your product — the people you wish to serve — are one of the goals of creating a community around your brand.

Ask Holly how a consultancy is created by Holly Howard that gives business owners the resources they need to expand while adhering to their mission. She approaches consulting from a culture-first perspective, and when considering community, she uses the following comparison.

"We want to view corporate culture as the ground [...] It serves as the basis, all of the sustenance, and the source of stability, according to Holly.

A community needs to change and improve.

One cannot "set and forget" about a community. There are times when your programmed needs additional categories or even a new functionality. It's crucial to change with your community if you want to keep things exciting and enjoyable for everyone. For more senior members, you may offer more levels, badges, or niche categories. You could elevate dependable people to a position of leadership.

You and your business should be on the road to success if you follow the following recipe. Do you have any more success advice? Comment on them to share them!

You want to produce content, not dialogue.

You may use the fresh tales, concepts, and experiences you gather from creating an online community in your blog, content marketing efforts, weekly email newsletters, book or online course creation. In reality, a community makes writing for yourself simpler since it provides you with more content.

Building an online community, however, might not provide you the same energy, excitement, or inspiration as it does to other artists if you find writing to be your most happy place (followed by counting the open rates or page views). After all, a community involves much more than just posting.

For your online community, select a platform.
You need a location for your online community to congregate. There are several approaches you may take here. Making a group on an existing social media site is the first option. The most typical choice is to start a Face book group.

Since many of your clients are already using those social networks and they are simple to use, this is the simplest route.

Another choice is to start your own forum. This forum may be a section of your website or a separate website. The fact that you have more control over analytics, data, and members is a benefit of this approach. However, since it's not a part of a well-known social media platform, you need to advertise it more.

Platform-related issues

Usability: Tools that are simple to use are more likely to be used. Make sure your platform can be accessed from a mobile device, has simple navigation, and is straightforward to sign in to.

Affordably priced: Many powerful community tools have a fee, even if your objective is to make the group free for members. Think about a tool that has a reasonable entry-level cost, doesn't take a cut of your revenues, and can scale with your company as it expands.

Goal alignment: After spending some time examining the rationale behind your group's existence, you need to have a solid idea of the characteristics that will enable you to achieve your objectives.

The owned platform, such as a community forum, comes next. All the advantages of a social media platform are available in this space, which is controlled by the company. However, you have a lot more control and freedom over how you engage with your users. You may control an owned community, for instance, if you start a blog or website with a forum or comment area for your visitors.

An owned community has advantages and disadvantages, much as free communities. This time, let's start with the drawback: From the audience's point of view, you're beginning from fresh. Owned communities provide you more control over the messaging for your business, but before customers are aware of your community,

Engage your staff in fostering a sense of community and culture

Without involving your staff, it is impossible to grow your corporate culture. It will be challenging to communicate your company's culture to an audience if your employees don't buy in.

"The outward community and the inside company culture should reflect each other [...] Employees, in my opinion, cannot provide an experience that they haven't had themselves. Therefore, we must ensure that we give the same experience internally if we are selling this experience to our community, says Holly Howard.

Kelly Phillips, co-founder of the restaurant collective Destination Unknown, supports the notion of building a fantastic internal culture that contributes to your exterior community by actively changing the culture of the service workers at her establishments.

The next stage is to build a fundamental plan on how to produce the value you are seeking after you have defined it. You must develop a fundamental strategy that outlines how to involve members, what subjects to emphasize, how to learn from and improve upon the many activities you will do. However, any strategy or plan needs to be quick and easy to implement. Though you must be realistic and choose urgent next actions that will help you verify your hypothesis and foster community, you must keep your eyes on the big picture (the overarching vision).

A brand community: what is it?

A brand community is, to put it simply, the epitome of brand loyalty. People that are emotionally involved in your business will buy from you, read your material, spread the word about you to their friends and family, and more.

However, brand awareness is not the same as a brand community.

Someone is not automatically a member of an engaged or even an engage able brand community just because they are aware of your brand or have made a purchase from it.

Instead, your brand community consists of individuals who like watching everything your brand does, who share your products/services and content with others, and who follow all of your material on social media.

Provide a Platform for Your Community

You'll need a platform where you can convey your message as well as a location where your community can congregate, communicate, and interact with both your startup and one another as you establish your prelaunch community.

Social is a clear example. For any startup, developing a strong social media presence is essential. This may be a brand-specific social media outlet, or you could start cultivating your community on your personal social media accounts.

The following social media platforms might be used: Face book groups, Reedit and subedits, Integra, Interest, Twitter, and YouTube. But not every social networking platform is made equal. For instance, Interest might not be the ideal if your business is mainly focused towards guys.

Conventions vary depending on the audience.
There may also be particular customs for particular audiences, which only serves to further complicate issues.

One recent candidate said that engagement had drastically decreased after switching from Discourse to their linked Sales force platform. Instead, developers had started using a member-hosted Slack channel.

Why did that take place?

Discourse provides features that developers prefer and are more familiar with since it is better for developers. Developers frequently employ Discourse, and this practice is commonly accepted. Natural inclinations are typically stronger than your own, thus you're likely to lose.

Similar to this, I recently dissuaded a game developer from establishing a forum where players could congregate and speak. Simply said, gamers no longer congregate there. They like Reedit, Discord, and other venues.

Find a goal that all the members can agree on.
The first step in creating year-round engagement is to define a sense of purpose that rings true every day of the year.

The chief product officer of Notified, Allie Magyar, started off as a meeting planner. She then founded her own event technology firm and partnered with Notified. She stated in a recent webinar co-hosted with the American Marketing Association, "As marketers, we are frequently trapped in a middle ground between what our firm wants to communicate against what customers are genuinely interested in. "We need to determine where those two intersect."

Before you try to find the intersection of the two highways, examine the many audience members who are sitting behind the wheel.

A brand community exists to benefit its members.

Managers frequently overlook the fact that customers are genuine individuals with diverse demands, interests, and obligations. Instead of generating revenue, a community-based brand develops customer loyalty by assisting customers in meeting their requirements. Contrary to what marketers would believe, however, the requirements that brand communities can fulfill go beyond just putting on a new persona or achieving prestige via brand identification. People join in communities for a number of reasons, including developing interests and skills, get emotional support and encouragement, and look for methods to help the larger good. Brand communities are a tool for members, not a goal in and of itself.

Why Is Workplace Community Important?

What's all the hoopla about when my team appears content enough and we're on schedule to meet our goals? It's an excellent query. On the surface, things could appear to be OK, but dig a little deeper, and frequently, the situation is quite different. More so in hybrid teams where computer displays can serve as impediments to fostering workplace communities.

A third of US workers say they have a sense of emptiness or alienation at work, according to

Cigna study. The poll provides information on how loneliness affects enterprises. The bottom line is being severely impacted by decreased productivity, rising illness, absenteeism, and turnover. The report's conclusion reads, "If we can start interacting with individuals at work more successfully.

Encourage Participation

Encourage conversations and increase engagement through various platforms as another strategy to create a community for your brand. Social media is a really potent tool and a fantastic method to communicate with the fans of your company. To grow the community, you may run polls and competitions or distribute a weekly or monthly newsletter to email subscribers. They may keep informed about everything going on in your company while also having fun in this way.

Imagine a neighborhood as a tree. For the tree to grow, you must plant the seeds and care for the roots each day. The seeds will just wither away without any care or water.

Online communities have been around for a while. A definitive reference on the step-by-step procedure for scaling and expanding a community is lacking, nevertheless.

There is information all over the place, but until today, nobody has truly let the beans on how to develop a community.

There are several factors that go into creating a successful community, including selecting the best platform, recruiting the initial few members, holding events, and moderation. We've got everything covered.

Do not forget that YouTube is a social networking platform.
It's simple to mistakenly refer to YouTube as only a website that hosts videos by believing that it is exclusively about videos.

It would be incorrect to see YouTube through such a lens, especially if you want to create a community.

You must keep in mind that while people may visit YouTube for content, they frequently return to a particular developing YouTube channel for the sense of community and connection if you want to be successful at creating a social media community on the platform.

Similar to how you would on any other social media platform, it is frequently possible to gauge this sense of community and connection by looking at interaction rather than views.

Why virtual communities should be preferred to social networks

People are turning away from social networks like Face book for a variety of reasons, including the spread of fake news and hate speech, privacy concerns, and ad fatigue.

Smart businesses have taken note of this development and developed exclusive communities where users can interact in a secure environment and build deeper relationships. Numerous businesses have even stopped using Face book for their advertising, such as Levi's and Hershey's, underscoring the trend away from social networks.

In fact, a wealth of research demonstrates that online communities may provide businesses a sizable competitive edge. Launching their network helped the power tool firm DEWALT save $6 million in research expenses.

Just why Create a Brand Community?

You may advance in so many ways with the aid of a brand community. It's the secret of effective marketing, first and foremost. Members not only assist in spreading the word but also provide your narrative a human touch. They give the community a personal touch and demonstrate to others that they, too, can be a part of it.

Second, you get immediate access to the people who really count – your target market. Your brand community may be used to test out new goods or services, get feedback on design concepts, and make more educated, client-focused choices.

It's crucial to keep in mind that there is already a community for your brand someplace.

Determine your objectives.

You need to create objectives for your entire business, not just for SEO, content, or social media, in hopes that you're sick of hearing me repeat it by this point. These objectives serve as the cornerstones of your company's strategy and direction (not merely in terms of marketing or community involvement).

You may set big, audacious objectives for your business that are more visionary, as well as more manageable, short-term project goals that you have in mind for creating things, constructing things, and just generally doing things you'd like to. Combine the two. You may organize and priorities these tasks when you get to the section when you're creating your strategy.

How can I advertise it?

Treat your community like you would any other product, and create a roadmap for future improvement.

I passionately believe in utilizing communities' capacity to foster a feeling of community and encourage sharing. Therefore, I believe it's crucial to maintain that at the centre of creating a community. People are more inclined to spread the news and recruit people to your cause if they feel like they belong.

With instance, I once served as a volunteer with Techs tars as an Organizer and Global Facilitator, hosting or facilitating Startup Weekends all around the world. My initial interest in companies and technology came from participating in my first Startup Weekend years ago.

Maintaining their participation is crucial after you have members in your online community. This can take many various shapes and will also depend on the individual member's motivations for wanting to take part and be an active member. The foundation of effective online community management in a research setting is providing your members with a wide range of activities. All of these actions go back to the objective you have for the neighborhood and your broader research projects. You are making surveys for the members to complete at the centre. One of the simplest methods to involve your members is through this.

Make use of social media.

We all like interacting with comparable individuals, and social media's accessibility and reach have made it possible for us to locate our tribes both domestically and abroad. Additionally, you get eager to interact with someone's material when you connect with them.

Parents may follow one another for their amusing stories and parenting advice. Fitness lovers share their workout plans and preferred clothing manufacturers. Foodies recommend restaurants and share delectable recipes with other food enthusiasts. The list keeps on.

Social media is the ideal platform for creating a strong community because users are already involved with these subcultures there. So, adapt to where your audience is.

Quality Should Precede Quantity

Create a set of standards for quality and abide by them. Although it may slow down community expansion, doing this will be in everyone's best interests. Additionally, it will foster a sense of exclusivity. You may frequently employ the quality factor as support for your community's promotion. Naturally, this means that you will occasionally have to say no. If this happens, be polite and explain your decision in detail. Setting up and upholding quality standards are an essential component of our service offering and for the consultants in our community given that we operate in the consulting industry.

Make use of brand ambassadors

Without going over budget, brand ambassadors may generate as much publicity for your company as influencers. Your brand may receive millions of free impressions thanks to the user-generated content your devoted followers can provide all while greatly expanding your community. Today's consumers like interacting with and promoting their favorite companies on social media. Additionally, ambassador programmers let your most ardent supporters promote your business and your items on your behalf. These devoted customers frequently get benefits like a welcome kit of brand merchandise, the opportunity to have their reviews posted on social media, and the option to organize sweepstakes. In exchange, they assist your company in growing.

Boost the lifetime value of each client

In today's era of customer-focused organizations, a company's success depends heavily on its ability to retain customers.

Many companies still believe that upwelling and talking to the client in emails would increase loyalty. When in fact building genuine connections based on trust is what loyalty is all about.

Private virtual communities encourage positive connections between peers and brands.

Customers may impact the path of the business through customer communities by exchanging opinions and thoughts on goods and services. This strengthens your relationship with them and increases their loyalty by turning them into an ally and crucial component of your company.

Consider the Correct Platforms

Finding the best platforms to implement your plan may be done after you've created the fundamentals of it. There are several options available here, including:

Social media is the best venue for creating a brand community, whether you utilize your own brand profile or start a group. You may quickly share user- and brand-generated content, initiate conversations, and spread a general buzz across the community with the potential for enormous reach.

Prizes and referrals: Encourage loyalty by giving out prizes like points for purchases, or exclusive deals and discounts for members.

Giving a financial incentive for each reference made is another way to promote community growth.

Execute every action in the step.

Start working on your plan now that it has been written. Ensure that the appropriate tracking and measurement is in place so that you can get information regarding your KPIs. Then stick to your plan and act consistently. People from your team (and from other teams) will keep approaching you with ideas that appear to be emerging but aren't really a part of the plan. This is your chance to tell them to "check the goals, baby" (as well as the strategy you've developed to get there). There will be situations (time-sensitive situations) that might require you to change your plan of action.

Companies that excel in community engagement

Though I haven't seen many businesses create communities that are particularly headed by product managers, I have seen several that are excellent at connecting with their fans in a variety of ways.

The word "community" nowadays has a wide range of meanings. For instance, I classify podcasts, blogs, and discussion forums as online communities. Like traditional in-person groups, they encourage interaction, spark dialogue, motivate action, and promote sharing.

Here are several companies that have developed fantastic communities, each of which tailored to the preferences and demands of its own audience:

The next phase in an online community management plan is to keep growing your community. You have established a community and have strong levels of involvement. Increasing the number of members you have will guarantee that you always hear new ideas from members. It will keep your community alive and active and prevent it from becoming stale over time.

Even the most successful communities experience times of attrition where they must rebuild their community and bring in new members. To ensure that you continue to get the knowledge you need for your study, it is crucial to carry on with this and include it into your plan for managing your online community.

Speak Your Community's Language

Every community has a founding member. You ought to be the best citizen in your neighborhood. You won't be able to comprehend their demands and provide them with genuine value-adding services if you don't grasp how the potential community members act, think, and feel. Given my own expertise as an independent consultant, creating a network of them was considerably simpler. I was able to comprehend the difficulties of being a consultant extremely well and add my own experiences to dialogues.

Every community is obviously unique, and its management must adjust appropriately, but no matter what kind of community you wish to create, you must learn their language.

For further control, use branded community platforms.

The first thing that comes to mind when people think about creating an online community is to utilize social media platforms as their platform; however, they have a number of limitations, which is why it is preferable to use branded community platforms. While free and offering the benefits of cross-service searches, social networking services like LinkedIn and Face book do not give you complete control over the website, which means that advertisements and other messaging may become a distraction. Branded community platforms, like Thinfic, are run completely by its owners, who have full control over branding, access, and content posting. Additionally, branded platforms don't have the distractions that are common on free ones.